THE REALITY OF
HOME-MADE WINE

Volume one

This short book is dedicated to all humans in the hopes that they all will learn to drink and eat healthier and live a much healthier and safer lives creating a situation where they will create a healthier and more productive version of ourselves.

G. C. Jones

2018

Chapter One

So, I Decided to Make Wine

So, I decided to make my own wine. There are several fruit trees on the property and I decided to use them for something other than bird food. This seemed to be a good choice since the birds just used the free food to shit all over everything, especially my vehicle and lawn-mower. I appreciate the fact that the birds are trying to compost, but personally I do not consider it to be compost if I have to wash it off of something I own.

So, I spent a few days doing some research on homemade wine and decided it should not be that complicated, and it turns out it isn't. There are many websites that will give detailed instructions and procedures that make it sound like it would be much simpler to just go to the local wine seller and buy a bottle of wine. But at this point, one must remember that making wine has been going on for many centuries in human history. Way back in ancient times, there was no local liquor store to pick up a bottle of wine. People made everything themselves, and wine was no exception. Which means in case society gets screwed up, or you go broke at some point, you should understand just how simple it really is to do.

I was originally going to use an empty one-gallon milk jug but the phrase 'jail-house wine' kept popping into my mind so I didn't use a plastic jug. One reason for this was I did not want the wine to have a plastic taste. Therefore, I bought three one-gallon glass jugs that came with what I call a double-bubble gas release device. It's a really cool device that allows gas produced by the wine to be released but keeps out the outside air or oxygen and everything else at the same time (including small bugs attracted to the smell of juice). It was a wise choice but for the record, one should also buy a cleaning brush that will reach the bottom of the jug because my local

Kroger's doesn't sell one at this time. While I was waiting on them to arrive, I decided to go ahead and start the process anyway.

On May 22, 201? I mixed up my first batch to start fermenting. I used 6 cups of fruit juice from Kroger's (or at least I thought it was real fruit juice, read the labels people), 3 cups of water (yes tap water was used), 1.5 cups of sugar, and one regular ¼ ounce package of plain yeast. All of this was mixed together in a one-gallon glass jug. I then used a rubber glove that did not have the powder on it (place close attention to the glove if you do it this way) and put a rubber band around the bottom of the glove holding it tight to the opening of the one-gallon glass jug.

I used a large spoon to stir it all together but I did not do that once I added the yeast. I added the yeast last so it would not start activating until I was ready to put the glove over the top of the jug. Looking back on the process after a few hours, I wished I had stirred up the mixture after I added the yeast. But time will tell if it makes a difference.

After a few hours, the glove was standing at attention. This shows the yeast is working and creating its gas and the fermenting process.

The glove was not severely pressurized but it was enough to make the glove stand up. Hopefully it will not blow off the top of the jug during the night while I am asleep. Once again, time will tell since it should take around 4 to 6 weeks for the process to be done. Once the glove loses pressure, or the yeast is no longer making the pressure in the glove; the first batch of wine will be done.

I am so enjoyed by the process that I am extremely glad that I ordered three one-gallon glass jugs that come with a double chamber air lock for the top of the bottle. This way I will not have to use the rubber glove once these arrive. I figure if I start a batch every few days or once a week and do a ¾ gallons each time; I should be able to dink my own homemade wine for pennies on the dollar at home and get flavors that I really like.

12:12 AM, I decided to shake the jug a little to stir up what appeared to be a layer of yeast looking foam on the top of the mixture. The entire mixture became cloudier after doing this and I believe it was a good idea to mix up the yeast that had not been activated by being mixed with the moisture. As long as it does not build up too much pressure in the rubber glove, it should be fine.

May 24, 201? update on wine. The rubber glove seems to be working just fine. It is more pressurized than it was a couple of days ago, but it still is not fully pressurized. The body of the glove is tight but the fingers are not near as tight, so it should take a little more pressure if needed. Mixture still looks cloudy but that was expected.

May 26, 201? update. I shook the bottle up in order to help mix in the sugar that was sitting on the bottom of the jar. Approximately thirty minutes later, the pressure inside the jar popped off the rubber glove from the top of the jar. I put another glove and rubber band over the top immediately hoping to not allow oxygen into the mix. It was a good thing I was close by when it popped off the rubber glove.

A few hours later, the glove is pressurized so tightly that I believe it could pop off the jar at any moment. I am still thinking about putting a tiny pin hole somewhere in the glove to see if it still will hold pressure but let excess pressure be released without letting oxygen. Time will tell.

At 3:45pm I decided to put the pinhole in the glove. It deflated in a few seconds and after it was about half flat I put a piece of scotch tape over the hole as best as I could. Hopefully this will allow pressure to build up and then release through the tape covered hole so it does not blow the glove off the top of the jar anymore. The glove started to inflate again immediately. Perhaps, the next time I decide to stir up the mixture to work the sitting sugar on the bottom back into the mix, I should wait until the time has expired and the glove has deflated on its own.

May 29, 201? update. The first batch seems to be doing fine at this point in time. The fermenting jugs with the double barrel ventilator arrived today. So, I started another batch in one of those new jugs using the same recipe that I used for the first batch. It will be interesting to see if this carbouy or ventilator works better and safer than the rubber glove.

May 30, 201? update. I have noticed that the second batch is working well. It has little bubbles working their way up through the carbouy every few seconds. This really makes me wonder about the balloon method because it would seem that the escaping gasses will not escape. Instead they should fall back into the wine mix and contaminate the entire jug.

Further research has yielded a better method of making wine. In the article, they stated the same thing I was wondering about and that is that with the glove or balloon method the gases do not escape and will ruin the wine. Therefore, I am going to transfer that first batch to one of the new jugs with a carbouy and hopefully save the batch from ruin.

The new article I fund on homemade wine can be easily found here; https://delishably.com/beverages/How_To_Make_Drinkable_Wine_In_Just_One_Week In case the link does not work I am going to copy and paste their procedural steps in with this writing.

"Ingredients:

- 1 cup of granulated sugar

- 1 gallon of whatever juice you like

- 1 packet of yeast

Instructions:

1. **Get Your Juice:** Buy grape juice. Grape is all I have ever experimented with, except for one batch of apple. Different

types of juice will probably produce different types of wine since each type of fruit has a different sugar content. I have used Sam's Choice and the Great Value brand from Wal-Mart, but you can use Welch's or any other brand.

2. **Get Around a Gallon of Juice:** I suggest one gallon, but you can use a smaller bottle. Look for "100% Juice" on the label. It will always say "from concentrate." Yeast will not do its job with preservatives present. Ascorbic acid and citric acid (Vitamin C) are ok. All grape juices are concentrated with water, so you'll never be able to get pure juice unless you squeeze the grapes yourself.

3. **Set the Juice Out so It Gets Room Temperature:** Juice should be at room temperature or slightly higher. If your juice is refrigerated, you need to leave it sitting out until it reaches room temp.

4. **Add Yeast:** Add one packet of active dry baker's yeast. Red Star and Fleichman's are the two brands I see the most in my local grocery stores. Do not stir. Do not add more yeast later; just this once. I generally follow this yeast rule about adding

yeast just once; however, I should say that in several batches I have refreshed the yeast by adding a teaspoon's worth. My advice is that if after about 3 days there is no more bubbling, add some more yeast. If this doesn't start some new bubbling activity, it is done, and you should allow this extra yeast time to settle to the bottom sediment. Finish by transferring to your final container.

5. **Bottle It and Leave Room for Air:** Screw the cap back on the bottle and loosen about one turn so air can escape. Fermentation produces carbon dioxide and needs to be able to vent from the bottle. I used to use a balloon, but other winemakers have suggested this should not be done because acids and other nasty things can build up in the balloon and fall back into the bottle. Makes sense to me.

6. **Keep an Eye on It:** Watch your project daily. After 3 days, check to see if it's still bubbling. If it has stopped, you can sample it now. If it's still bubbling, just keep checking it daily until it isn't bubbling anymore. If you really can't see any bubble action, put your ear to it and listen.

When the Wine Is Finished:

1. **Find a Glass Container:** When you are satisfied that your wine is ready to drink, transfer the wine from your fermentation container/original bottle to another clean container of plastic or glass. Old, sterilized glass wine bottles are perfect.

2. **Transfer Wine Without Upsetting the Sediment:** When transferring the wine, use a plastic funnel. Once you've tipped the wine to pour, DO NOT turn the bottle back up straight but keep pouring until you're finished. There is sediment left over at the bottom that contains acids and impurities. If you keep tipping the bottle, you'll stir up the sediment and ruin the wine. Siphoning with a hose would be just as good or even better, just leave the end of the hose an inch or so above the sediment to avoid sucking it out with the good stuff.

3. **Refrigerate and Enjoy:** After bottling your brew, it is suggested that you refrigerate but leaving out at room

temperature is ok as long as your room temperature is not really hot. Keep out of direct sunlight.

Please drink responsibly and enjoy the fruits of your labor.

A Bit More Info

This Recipe Stands Out Because It's Simple: Ok, there are tons of homemade wine recipes on the internet. This is the lazy man's recipe that only requires three ingredients available at just about any grocery store, and your wine will be ready to drink in one week or less. The taste will improve, and the alcohol content will increase if you let it age longer. But it's not necessary. I presently have some aging in the fridge, and I tell you, it has a very strong alcohol aroma and a real kick. I actually don't care that much for wine but like the challenge of making it from such simple means. It has to be better than Mad Dog 20/20 or Thunderbird or the nasty hooch prisoners make in their toilets.

Juice Produces Ethanol, Not Methanol: Making homemade wine, or alcohol in general, is simple because of the simple fact that yeast converts sugar to ethanol (alcohol). There is a misconception that drinking homemade brew is not safe, but that's only if you drink methanol. Brewing with fruit juices and yeast cannot produce methanol. It can only produce ethanol.

This Can Be Done in as Little as Three Days: My attempts at wine making usually take around 7 days, but some people who have tried this method have reported that the fermentation (yeast completely stopped making bubbles) stopped in about 3 days. So this method can actually produce wine with a moderate alcohol content in about 3 days.

You Might Need to Add Sugar: Since this fermentation method produces wine that isn't very sweet (because the yeast converted all the sugar in the juice to alcohol), I am updating my recipe by saying that you should add one cup of granulated or cane sugar or corn syrup to a one gallon batch or half a cup to a half gallon batch before adding the yeast. This might produce a sweeter wine, if that's what you want. It might be best to pour the juice into a large saucepan and heat it up slightly (not over 110 degrees F) so the sugar will dissolve properly. Then pour it back into the bottle using a funnel and allow to cool to room temperature.

A Hydrometer Will Tell You the Alcohol Content: I'm not sure of the alcohol content of this brew, but you could buy a hydrometer to measure it. They are cheap and readily available online or at any brewer's store.

Get Winemaking Yeast, If Possible: If you live in a city that has a home-brewing supply, I advise buying yeast made just for winemaking. Active baker's yeast from grocery stores works ok, but the real winemaking yeast is formulated better for wine, doesn't peter out as fast, and will add a few days to my "one week" method. I have never experienced a "bread smell" using baker's yeast" (Wino, 2017).

At 1:48pm on May30, 201? I transferred the contents of batch one to a glass jug with a carbouy. It had a strong alcohol smell and had very little sediment on the bottom of the first jug when emptied. Hopefully the carbouy will start to show bubbling in a few minutes. Otherwise I will have to either add more yeast which could affect the taste a little, or just pour it out and start over with a new batch.

At 3:33pm I noticed that the first batch that had now been transferred to the new jug still had not built up any pressure. In my mind this means that the yeast had done all it was going to do. It could be strained and drank at this point but I felt that there was a lot more sugar left in the container. Therefore, I added one more package of yeast to the mix. My research shows that the preservatives in the punch will cause the yeast to not perform as well, so I felt this was needed to get the first batch to where it needs to be.

6-05-201? update. I have noticed over the last two days that the pressure in both the older mix and the newer mix has been going down according to the double bubbler vent. The latest batch still has bubbles moving on the surface so obviously it is still working off. However, there is very little activity in the first or older batch.

Therefore, I decided I could wait no longer and I had to try a sample of the first batch. I poured about two or three shots out into a red solo cup and then put one shot in a shot glass. Since it was warm or at room temperature I knew it would not taste as good as it would if it was cold. But what the hell, I wanted to taste it, so I did at 7:49pm.

It tasted better than I thought it might but not as good as I believed and hoped it would. But it was good and seems to have a better kick and smoothness than anything else I have drunk in quite a while. I can feel a small buzz just from that one shot. It is now 8:04 and I think I will have another shot from the red solo cup I placed in the refrigerator earlier. So, so far so good, let's see what happens next, lol!!

OK, one thing I have to add after walking back into the kitchen where both batches of wine are sitting, is that now that I have poured a little out of the first batch and put the double bubble back on top, the bubbler now has plenty of action. As if the pouring out or stirring up has helped the process to continue. The really strange part is that the second batch which is still untouched is now bubbling again as well. OK, I did shake the jar up a little when I got some out of the first batch but not much!

After the second shot, I am starting to feel as if I had a swig of moonshine. So, this home-made wine thing could be a good thing. If this keeps up, I will not have any need to buy beer anymore, just fruit juice every few weeks and wait until it is done. A few shots a day and Ta-Da good buzz rolling without all the beer LOL!!

I also should add that I did have two beers before I started this process today. It was my last two beers in the fridge and I did not want to spend anymore money on beer at this time. After all, saving money and still being able to drink a little is one of the main points that got me started on the home-made wine making process. Now, I think I will go get that third shot of home-made wine!!

06-07-201? update. So, I forget to add that I took 4-6 more shots last night and everything was fine. It does taste better when chilled but can be drank either way hot or cold. Today I have about 6-8 shots chilled in the fridge and will be taking shot samples throughout the day. Since both batches have seemed to stop bubbling even when shaken up, I believe both batches are about ready to chill and drink as needed for medicinal purposes only!!

So, after a few shots I decided to say 'fuck the dumb shit' and packaged up the first batch. I took it out of the jug and packaged it at 4:20pm. I stored it in an empty half gallon milk jug that I had cleaned out earlier in the week for this occasion. I got enough out of the jug to completely fill the milk jug. Since I have been sipping on this batch for a few days I thought that was a pretty good haul from my FIRST batch of home-made wine.

There was some sludge in the bottom of the jug, some would call it thicker stuff; but whatever you call it I decided not to save or use that part of the batch. I then put it in the fridge to chill for a few days but still took a shot or two as required to remain safe at heart LOL!!

06-09-201? update. I have put some of the wine in my cup so it could get colder in a smaller part of the fridge and it seems to have been an excellent idea. But I have noticed somewhat of a sour taste to the wine. Kinda' makes me think that I should no longer add any water to the batches in the future. Pure juice is the way to go from now on when making home-made wine.

This evening I took my drinking cup and filled it up ¾ of the way to the top. I then took three small spoonful's of sugar and added it to the cup. It was a VERY GOOD idea!! This stuff is great, it tastes good, has a good buzz, and I realize how important it is to get another batch started. I still have the second batch working off, but it isn't doing much bubbling anymore even when I shake the jug. So, it could be about ready to package and chill.

If I package the second batch at this time, I will have three empty jugs not making any wine. Therefore, I think I will wait until I either get another batch going, or drink all of the first batch before I package and chill the second batch. So, until then or the next update, CHEERS!! (This is where one can hear the glasses clinking and hear everyone drinking some good home-made wine!!)

06/10/201? update. So, after a few glasses of the first batch it was nearly gone and I was as drunk as if I had drunk 12 beers. So today I decided to go ahead and package up the second batch. Since it only received one package of yeast it should be ready. There are no more bubbling and the double bubble device has lost pressure. So, at 5:45pm today I packaged it up. I got one half gallon plus about two glasses in another jug. Now, I am truly ready to mix up another batch or three while I drink on what I have packaged up.

Chapter Two

Honey Wine

06/10/201? is the start of chapter two or how to make home-made honey wine. Since honey is so sweet, sugar should not be needed for this recipe. I got the idea from a recipe I found on the Internet. The recipe and article I found is;

"In the DEAR MOTHER section of MOTHER EARTH NEWS No. 3, Gary Dunford asked if it's possible to make wine at home without buying $40 worth of equipment. The answer is yes.

I started making wine with stuff I could scrounge while living in a one room apartment in the city. Following are my own Super Simple directions. They're guaranteed to drive dedicated winemakers up a wall but they do produce results. Anyway, they're a beginning and beginnings are the most important part.

You can make wine out of almost any fruit. In fact, you can make it from just about anything that grows. I have used grapes, pears, peaches, plums, blackberries, strawberries, cherries and—my favorite—honey. Honey wine is called Mead. The so-called wine of the gods. It's cheap, easy and good. Here's how:

Homemade Wine Recipe

Get a gallon jug, preferably glass but plastic will do. Clean it out good. Smell it. Someone may have kept gasoline in it. Wash the jug with soap (NOT detergent), rinse with baking soda in water and—finally—rinse with clear water.

Put a pint and a half to two pints of honey in the jug (the more honey, the stronger the wine), fill with warm water and shake.

Add a pack or cake of yeast—the same stuff you use for bread—and leave the jug uncapped and sitting in a sink overnight. It will foam at the mouth and the whole thing gets pretty sticky at this point.

After the mess quiets down a bit, you're ready to put a top on it. NOT, I say NOT, a solid top. That would make you a bomb maker instead of a wine maker.

What you have to do is come up with a device that will allow gas to escape from the jug without letting air get in. Air getting in is what turns wine mixtures into vinegar.

One way to do the job is to run a plastic or rubber hose from the otherwise-sealed mouth of the jug, thread the free end through a hole in a cork and let the hose hang in a glass or bowl of water. Or you can make a loop in the hose, pour in a little water and trap the water in the loop to act as a seal.

Now put your jug of brew away about two weeks until it's finished doing its thing. It's ready to bottle when the bubbles stop coming to the top.

Old wine bottles are best. You must use corks (not too tight!) to seal the wine as they will allow small amounts of gas to escape. The wine is ready to drink just about any time.

You can use the same process with fruits or whatever, except that you'll have to extract the juice and, maybe, add some sugar. You'll also find that most natural fruit will start to ferment without the yeast and will be better that way.

Once you've made and enjoyed your first glass of wine, no matter how crude, you'll be hooked" (Miller, 1970).

In case you are wondering why I added the exact articles or recipes that I found and used as a guide, it is because I wanted you to be able to read the exact article and be able to use which ever method works best for you and your own specific taste of wine.

Around 9:30 this evening I started this third batch of wine. I used a good clean one-gallon milk jug, added warm water until it was about ¾ of the way to the top. I then added 24 oz. of Grade A 100%pure clover honey from Kroger's. Then a package of yeast and put the double bubble device on top of the jug. I have left it in the sink for now in case if foams over like it said in the article. I also see why they mentioned shaking up the jug because the honey went straight to the bottom of the jug. Hopefully the yeast will still get to it and ferment into wine.

I did shake the jug a little but not much because I did not see it doing any good for the mixture. After about 15 minutes, there was a foam starting to build up on top of the mixture and the handle of the jug was full of foam. The double bubble device was also starting to bubble. So, it seems to be starting the fermenting process immediately.

06-12-201? update. The double bubble device is bubbling faster than either of the two first batches ever did. At first, I was a little concerned about it but it should be fine. I was also concerned about all the honey being on the bottom of the jug. But it seems to be getting eat up by the yeast because there is less and less honey on the bottom of the jug as time goes on.

06-13-201? update. The honey batch is still bubbling away at a nice steady pace. The honey that was piled up on the bottom is almost gone. So, it apparently does not matter if part of the mix is sitting on the bottom.

I also mixed up two more batches to ferment today. I put one gallon of Ocean's Spry Cranberry-grape juice, 1.5 cups of sugar, and one package of yeast in the first one at 12:30pm. The second one I mixed up today is similar to the first two I did when I first started this adventure. The second one contains one gallon of Hawaiian Punch, 1.5 cups of sugar, and one package of yeast. As you can see both are similar to the first ones but without the water added.

06-15-201? update. I noticed this morning after I woke up that the Hawaiian Punch mix had stop bubbling. In fact, the bubbler had actually started working in REVERSE. I have no idea why but it did make me think that the yeast did not activate properly. I took the bubbler off to release pressure but after a few minutes it went back to working in reverse. Therefore, I added another package of yeast at 7:45am and it started working properly in a matter of a few minutes.

06/20/201? update. All of the three batches are doing good since the last update. The Hawaiian Punch and the grape ones are bubbling at a good steady pace. The honey baych has slowed down to the point of barely bubbling at all. It is so slow that I am contemplating bottling it up. But, I believe I will wait a day or so before I do.

At 7:30pm I decided I had waited long enough. Since there were very few bubbling actions in the honey batch, it is time to package it up and start drinking again. I poured the contents of the honey batch into two half gallon jugs. Each jug was filled about ¾ of the way to the top. I then filtered the wine through a Brita water filter to get rid of any contaminants. This was a pain in the ass but it turns out it could have been a good idea. It filtered out so much it made the color lighter. Therefore, I believe it is a good idea to use the Brita filter.

After it is done filtering I am going to put it in the fridge to get cold and hopefully I will be able to drink some after I get a quick shower. It smells good and looks like beer, but we shall see. It only fermented for 10 or 11 days but since some recipes stated it only took a week, I figured it was close enough to drink and have some fun bragging to my friends about how I can get just as drunk for pennies on the dollar all the while drinking something I made myself and is safer and healthier than store bought crap.

It tastes pretty good, very similar to store bought sour wine. So, I added three spoons of sugar into my glass as I have done on previous batches and it is now very good!! I now have enough to sip on until the next batch is ready to package, chill, and drink.

I went ahead and started another batch using Hawaiian Punch. This batch is made up of ¾ gallon of punch, 1.5 cups of sugar, one red solo cup of water to activate the yeast, and one package of yeast. Hopefully since I added one cup of water to activate the yeast, another package of yeast will not be needed. But, only time will tell.

It isn't bubbling as quick as other juices, and it is doing the same thing the last batch of punch did by working or pulling pressure backwards. If it is still doing this in a few hours I will simply go ahead and add another package of yeast as I have had to do with all other batches using punch as the juice.

06/22/201? update. The latest batch of wine does not want to ferment as it should be. Therefore, once again I will have to add another package of yeast to the Hawaiian Punch mixture. Perhaps I should try not to use Hawaiian Punch anymore. But it does taste good, so we will see.

06/23/201? update. So, I got a few tastes of the Hawaiian Punch mixture last night after I finished drinking all the honey wine, and it was good. Therefore, I will go ahead and package up this batch so I will have some ready to drink when I need it. Now I just have to get more juice so I can start the next batch.

I believe I have got you far enough through the experimental process of making your own wine. SO, I will not be adding anymore updates except maybe to tell you how good I feel when I am drinking my own home-made wine. Just kidding, this is the end of my notes on the subject. If you need to know more or need advice,

feel free to ask!! Have a Nice Day, and I hope you enjoy your own

version of home-made wine just as much as I have. Thank you again

for reading this far!!

Chapter Three

Favorite Flavors

09/19/201? update. So, here it is roughly three months later and I am still making my own homemade wine. I am no longer experimenting with flavors. I did enjoy my short trip through the flavors, but ended up deciding to just make my favorite flavor most of the time. As it turns out, my favorite flavor is fruit punch, a simple mixture of several fruit flavors. Me second favorite is blackberry juice and I will be making more of that just not very often, and even less often in the grape flavor.

I still have not obtained a device to test the 'proof' of my homemade wine, but according to the effects of drinking just a glass or two, it might not be a major requirement (written as I am taking another good sip from a 16 oz glass of freshly made wine). Sometimes the effects are the only 'proof' that is needed, lol!

Once I can get enough extra funds to get some wine bottles and corks, I am going to make different batches of flavors and bottle one of each. In this manner I will be able to test the long-term effects of my wine. In many cases, wine will get better with age when stored properly. Once it has time to decanter, it does get better with age. In just a week or two, it can get much better to taste and in proof, or at least the last batch I tested for two weeks was much better.

I have also noted that it is much better to use pure juice when making wine. Pure juice will ferment quicker and be good and strong. Fruit juice, like what I personal favor, usually has preservatives and such in it and will require an extra step to properly ferment. In order to properly ferment fruit juice with preservatives and such in it, you will need to add a second package of yeast around two or three days after initially starting the batch of wine when making it in one-gallon batches as I have been doing through-out this whole book.

I would also like to mention at this time I forgot to mention one of my real favorite flavors 'Honey-Wine'! Home-made wine made from honey is really, really good. However, in case you have not noticed the price of honey at virtually any farmers market or local grocery store, it is really expensive. I am related to several people that have their own bee hives and sell honey. Yes, they do give some away in small amounts but that is usually to the elderly and under privileged. Which means they are not going to give it away to me so I can make wine out of it and I do not blame them one bit. I would feel the same way they do if it were my hives and honey.

Usually when most people make wine from honey (also known as 'mead') they usually add water. Where you get the water from, and how much water you add will directly affect the taste of the wine. The better quality of the water, and the less one uses of it, the better the quality of wine will be produced, plus it will be stronger with less water.

Therefore, it is easy to see why 'mead' is much more expensive to make. Since it foams up when fermenting I would suggest only making a half gallon at a time in a one-gallon container. This way you leave room for the batch to foam up without over-flowing out of the one-gallon container.

One can obtain a gallon of wine online for around $12 to $15 plus shipping. But that is not a locally made wine that supports local beekeepers and your own local economy, plus it is probably much safer for you to consume. You will never create any bad karma by supporting your local farmers and neighbors like you want them to support you if you were selling your own honey, or wine.

The bottom line is, pick your own favorite flavor, just make sure you understand what is required to make that flavor no matter what it is made from. Use quality ingredients, you will be much happier in the long run, trust me on that, there is no bigger let-down from making your own home-made wine than to get a batch that you want to through away after you waited two weeks to taste it.

One of the main reasons to make your own home-made wine is very simple. YES, I probably should have mentioned this earlier but consider it a reward for those that actually read this all the way through. Since I started making, and drinking, my own home-made wine- I have not have one hangover. That is a true fact, and the main reason everyone should have at least one batch of wine of their own fermenting in a back room somewhere.

Yes, I have been known to wake up still drunk from the night before due to drinking in excess just a little, but there was no hangover, no headache from alcohol, no usual hangover sickness, just a healthier feeling and a desire for breakfast, and then to sober up.

This leads me to believe that one of the main reasons that a hangover occurs is because of the chemicals that is put in 'store bought' alcohol. If you read the label on what you buy, or what the government allows you to buy, it is easy to see a list of chemicals in the liquid you are drinking. It is these chemicals that create the hang-over you will experience when drinking. Therefore, why not make your own without the chemicals, or aka something with more kick and no chemicals that will give you a hang-over?

Sounds pretty darn simple to me! Common sense should tell anyone that your own all-natural home-made wine is safer than a more expensive, store bought alcohol that has a list of chemicals that the government requires to be added for 'your safety'. If these chemicals create pain for you, then they are not really there for your safety.

BTW, I bought three more glass one-gallon jugs for fermenting my own home-made wine. I now have a total of six glass one-gallon jugs in a constant process of making my own home-made wine for personal consumption of course.

Chapter Four

Financially Speaking

Another one of the main reasons that started me down this road to making my own home-made wine is due to my personal financial situation, also known as, I didn't have the money to buy alcohol, whether it be cheap beer or cheap vodka, I was simply too broke to get drunk and that in itself is a sad state of mind to be in no matter who you are at any point in time in what we commonly know of as America.

If you think about the fact that a simple 30 pack of Busch beer (sorry Busch, I only used you as an example because I have bought many 30 packs of your beer and drank them all, and if I were to buy another 30 pack at this time it would probably be a 30 pack of Busch Beer) cost on the average $20 by the time one adds the cost of taxes and gasoline.

If one buys on average, two 30 packs of beer a week, and that can be a generalized average for someone that likes to have a cold beer or two on a daily basis; then the average weekly cost for that habit is about 440 a week. That works out to be on average to be .67 cents a beer. That doesn't sound like much until one looks at the cost of a gallon of home-made wine. Take a moment to notice that the price previously noted for beer was per 16 ounce can of beer.

In order to make one gallon of wine, as I currently make it, it cost about $2.99 per gallon of fruit juice, about $2 for a bag of sugar that will produce about four or five gallons of home-made wine, and about $1.40 for three packages of simple bread yeast (two of which will be used as previously mentioned per gallon of fruit punch home-made wine). Also there is the cost of the glass jugs and the double-bubble devices to fit onto the top of the one-gallon jugs, but once those are bought, they no longer figure into the equation of cost of production.

Therefore, for about $4 a gallon, versus $10 to $15 a gallon for beer, one can easily see it is much cheaper to make your own home-made wine versus a much more expensive drink that will absolutely give you a hang-over and cost more money to have that hang-over. When you could have a home-made drink that is safer, chemically speaking, and does not include pain as a 'side-effect', and taste the way you want it to taste, also known as 'it comes in your own personal favorite flavor'!

Another side of the financial equation is whether or not you should sell any of your home-made wine to your friends. This should be thought about and researched very closely. In most states there are laws against doing this and could get you put in jail. So, research the laws closely in your own state, and if possible, ask an attorney. If you do not have an attorney, or at least have one on retention, then perhaps you should not start selling your own home-made wine.

Chapter Five

Decanting

The decanting process should be taken seriously. Granted, your home-made wine can be drunk without decentering, but once you try it after it has had time to decanter you will want to do it all that way.

"Decanting wine is essentially the process of pouring (decanting) the contents from one vessel (typically a bottle) into another vessel (typically a decanter). Usually the wine is then served from the decanter, but sometimes in a restaurant it is decanted back into the original bottle for service" (Gorman, 2011).

"Not every wine needs decanting. Many of us associate decanting with older vintage port wines or aged Bordeaux – wines that throw off a lot of sediment as they age. Decanting separates the wine from the sediment, which not only would not look nice in your glass, but would also make the wine taste more astringent. Slowly and carefully decanting the wine ensures that the sediment stays in the bottle and you get a nice clear wine in the decanter, and subsequently in your glass.

A second and more everyday reason to decant is to aerate the wine. Many young wines can be tight or closed on the nose or palate. As the wine is slowly poured from the bottle to the decanter it takes in oxygen, which helps open up the aromas and flavors. Highly tannic and full-bodied wines benefit most from this – wines such as Cabernet Sauvignon, Cabernet blends, Syrah, and Syrah blends" (Gorman, 2011).

So, one can easily see that the main reason to decant your own home-made wine to let things settle to the bottom of the container. If you do not have an expensive filtering device then this can be an important step in the process to enhance flavor and drink-ability for some people.

This affect of decanting is done when removing the wine from the fermenter itself. If you remember there was a sludgy looking substance in the bottom of the fermenter. When you keep that sludgy part from entering your product, you are decanting the wine. After you make a few gallons of your own wine, this will become more apparent.

Therefore, decanting is a necessary step in the process, and does take place at several points in the process. The final decanting process in my process simply consist of putting the wine back in the original fruit juice container, writing the date on the container, placing it in the refrigerator, and waiting a few days. Placing your wine in a refrigerator can slow down any fermenting process that might be taking place, regardless of how little of it there is, let it decanter, and keep it cold for sipping purposes.

Chapter Six

In Conclusion

In conclusion, it is safe to say, making your own home-made wine is well worth your time. No, it will not give you a hang-over when done correctly. Yes, you could wake up still slightly drunk when done correctly. The choice is up to you and your own taste, self-control, personal drinking habits (which will re-adjust once you taste your own version of wine), and state of mind at any given moment in your own personal history.

So, the answer to the main question is YES, you should make your own home-made wine. It is not the answer because it is healthier for you to drink. It is not the answer because it taste better. It is not the answer because you will no longer have a hang-over as some people have become accustomed to having. It is not the answer because it could save you hundreds of dollars a month. It IS the answer because you CAN make your own home-made wine!! Enjoy your next drink my friend!!

References

Gorman, M., (2011), *Decanting Wine: When and Why to Decant Wine | Kitchn*. Retrieved from,

https://www.thekitchn.com/do-you-have-a-wine-145131

Miller, G., (1970), *A Cheap and Easy Homemade Wine Recipe - Real Foods – MOTHER EARTH NEWS*. Retrieved from, https://www.motherearthnews.com/real-food/homemade-wine-recipe-zmaz70sozgoe

Wino, (2017), *How to Make Wine in Just One Week | Delishably.* Retrieved from, https://delishably.com/beverages/How_To_Make_Drinkable_Wine_In_Just_One_Week